Mothers and Fathers, Sons and Daughters

poems by

James Hochtritt

Finishing Line Press
Georgetown, Kentucky

Mothers and Fathers, Sons and Daughters

*in memory of Robert Anthony Mello who always understood
and with love and respect to my wife Joyce, the toughest person I know*

Copyright © 2025 by James Hochtritt
ISBN 979-8-89990-003-7 First Edition
All rights reserved under International and Pan-American Copyright Conventions. No part of this book may be reproduced in any manner whatsoever without written permission from the publisher, except in the case of brief quotations embodied in critical articles and reviews.

Publisher: Leah Huete de Maines
Editor: Christen Kincaid
Cover Art: James Hochtritt
Author Photo: Megan Ronio
Cover Design: Elizabeth Maines McCleavy

Order online: www.finishinglinepress.com
also available on amazon.com

Author inquiries and mail orders:
Finishing Line Press
PO Box 1626
Georgetown, Kentucky 40324
USA

Contents

Bakersfield, California 1933	1
On The Road To Forget	2
Searching	3
Inscriptions	4
Purple Heart	5
Organic	6
Photo	7
Strangers	8
Near San Tomás Aquino Creek	10
Confession	11
Sunnybrae	13
Anamnesis	16
Post Card	17
After Hours	18
Prima Facie	19
Rosabel's Tio In The San Joaquin Valley	20
Out Of Limits	21
Witness	22
Healing	23
Sometimes	24
Silhouette Of Mato Tipila	26
Before Panel 17W—Line 3	28
That Year	29
Closing Up Shop	30
Ephemeral	31
Hope Springs Eternal	32
Alice Drive	33
Chain-link Fence	34

In The Aftermath Of Ashes 35
Noa's Savta 37
Sanctuary 38
House 41
Other Side Of The Tracks 42
Frida 44
Bonfire 45
Archaeologist 46
Among Other Things 47
In The Shadow Of The Mission And The Monastery 49
Last Respects At The Grandparents' Farm 50
Mirrors 52
Beyond The Reach 53

But I'll know my song well before I start singin'
Bob Dylan

Bakersfield, California 1933

Along the vast expanse of the flat plain
Where the dark slate sky of dusk
Intersects the black line of the horizon,
Pastel evaporation of the wind-dusted day
Dissolves into a fog of clouds,
And the scent of imminent rain
Blends with the songs of southbound birds.

Near the eastern hills outside of town
The toxic odor of an invisible gas
Hangs heavy on the soil,
As pump jacks, skeletal derricks
And storage tanks of the oil fields
Serve their purpose around the clock,
Synonyms of progress and profit.

Aloneness is not a ghost here
Or even a dim figment of a desperate imagination,
But a palpable taste
As stark as the whiteness of bleached bones,
An all-embracing emptiness
As blank as a winter night,
Portentous and without stars.

There is no room for weakness here
In the aftermath of ashes,
And the expectations that parents hold
For themselves and for their children
Are carefully worded or completely hidden,
Confluence of grim truth and tenderness
And that not swallowed by disappointment.

There persists only the dignity of the human spirit here
Distilled down to its fragile essence,
Stubborn resistance of women and men
Defiance against mortality,
That their living and dying should not be insignificant
If not in the hearts of their fellow man
Then at least in the eyes of hope.

On The Road To Forget

No one knows my name, here and now, back road stranger,
Wind blowing my hair this way and that,
Rain starting to fall, fragrance of cypress and magnolia,
Deafening bellow of semis,
Diesel beasts devouring air.

I'm a lone thumb marooned in the southern dusk,
Curses of soldiers eating corn bread and beans,
Confederacy in the review mirror.
I'm a stick stuck in the mud, nowhere hobo
In the isolation of circumstance.

Sound of a hungry owl, screech of brakes,
Piercing scream, unsettling and unnerving,
Freight train whistle in the distance,
I puff on a hand rolled cigarette
Pondering Jefferson Davis, land of cotton.

I'm an exile shrugged off and forgotten
By disgusted lover, close tie, disgruntled relative.
I munch on one last stale doughnut
Bought one week ago on the shores of Lake Charles
Wash it down with a warm Coke,
Stamp my feet to circulate blood,
Button the top button of my ragged coat
To keep away the cold.

Disquieting night of ghosts and lost causes,
Landscape of monuments and unmarked graveyards,
Breaking bones and humid fields full of whip cracks,
Mournful sobs of mothers,
Babies dying in the dirt.

I swear I can hear the echoes,
Weeping of the willows,
Breathing of the Spanish moss.
Am revealed in this nightmare, a 'Yankee'
Haunted by the constant vigil of barking dogs,
History, the hunter, tracking me
Snapping at my heels.

Searching

The inlet of your smile always softens my return.
In the estuary of your strength, sanctuary,
Tenderness to fend off an emptiness which threatens to overwhelm.
This desperate searching is wearing me down, my ability to think clearly.
Certainly we should have found some tiny shred of evidence:
A shoe, a torn piece of blue cloth, the scarf she wore, the hat she had on,
But no such luck for the frantic.
We are an army of the haunted cast upon a landscape,
Disheartened shadows beneath autumn sky.

It's been nearly a week since she disappeared
And fear of what we find if we find anything at all
Has torn my hope from its moorings.
Stoicism of the cops I can handle, but not the mother's loss,
Father's contorted expression frozen into a mask…
I want to be a saint, soothe their pain, bring their child back,
But I cannot walk on water like it's claimed that Jesus did.
I wander home through a hazy fog of dusk
Kick muddy boots to the floor and stare at the glassy bay.

I'm no angel, and the world beyond my window offers no comfort or peace
And the Novocain of this whiskey is not nearly enough.
Candleglow, caring arms, kind words,
Let down your hair and beautiful light fall gently on my face.
We are so fortunate, you and I, and tomorrow is not far off.
Let us close our eyes and dream, somehow reconcile our faith,
Do what it is when people pray in spite of disbelief.

Inscriptions

Their collective presence is recollected from the soft thaw of time,
Humble images reconstructed from numerous seasons of distance,
Subconscious now illuminated for better judgment.
Their fevers and aspirations forever simmer in our bloodlines,
This generation of sons who became our fathers,
Mostly Mexican, Irish, Portuguese, and Italian,
Devoted Catholics to the sacraments and traditions.

Optimistic offspring of industrious immigrants,
Uneducated men whose backs and hands bore their burdens.
Veterans armed with G.I. loans and post-war expectations,
They courted their sweethearts at theaters and beaches,
In beat up cars on moonlit drives.
Ordinary men wearing wounds and scars, bloody knuckles and tattoos,
Casualties of accidents and alcohol, tumors and lupus.

Yesterdays of their rage, gruff tenderness, somnambulant memories
Resurrected in old postcards and photographs.
Mysterious ontology in their eyes, visible physiology of their fears.
With elbows propped on the hieroglyphic wood of smoky bars,
They cracked raw eggs into foamy beers,
Cauterized desperation with cynicism and anecdotes, deadpan humor,
Shouldered family histories that were not their fault.

Work weathered and withered men, ballplayers and welders,
Bricklayers and insomniacs, enigmas, taciturn men of sweat and silence.
Cigarettes dangling from encouraging mouths,
They built monuments for us boys out of sandlots and spit,
Hoisted us to fountains we could not reach.
With burnished dreams and pride concealed in stoic throats,
Rejoiced in our exploits neutered glories of their youth.

Fragile pathos of their failures, hard-bitten humilities,
They drove us hard to protect us from their mistakes.
If they made love to our mothers, we never knew, never heard,
And we forgave them anyway, their weakness, as only innocence could.
In the sprawling monotony of pastel suburbs we buried these men with praise,
And understood in eulogies, by comparisons, ourselves,
Ambiguities more profound than any infallible truths.

Purple Heart

Bright sunlight in the window
Cannot warm the chill of night sweats.
She shivers still in the aftermath of a shower,
Beaded dewdrops across her shoulders.

What happened to the girl who giggled as she dressed,
Made forts with her friends out of blankets and chairs,
Dropped out of high school to help out her dad?

She stands bent before the glass,
First eyeliner, then foundation, then lipstick applied
Ever so carefully, blotting her lips to seal the color.

She draws back to better focus on her image in the mirror,
Red stream of a scar that starts between her breasts
And runs across the soft meadow of her belly
To just above the apex of her pelvis.

Decades down the road lost in thought
She stares daydreaming and distracted,
Imagines her reflection captured in the clear water of a bath
As she washes two feet with her tenderness and tears
And dries the tiny toes with her hair.

Organic

It struggled in powder on top of a pond, drifts up to its chest,
Frost covering its hindquarters, cloudy air from the exhalation
Of flared nostrils, blood red bubbles foaming from its mouth.

Motionless I hunched on half-frozen haunches, vicarious
Voyeur concealed in woods, white steam rising from dark water
And mass, its ebony exhaustion of bone and muscle.

Accomplice to its agony, hypnotized I focused on its black eyes
And calamity, its panicked whines and gurgles, guttural snorts,
Throes of its violent thrashing snapping icicles off branches.

Bewildered terror of its dying reverberated and echoed
Off bushes and stones, scattered birds to flight, contrast
Of stunned surprise against the backdrop of the meadow.

Wooded silence, my labored breath, shards of ice like broken glass
As it vanished below the surface, disbelieving witness
Of the heavenly sky, cathedral falling of the sacred snow.

Photo

It's an old photograph,
Image of a man on his knees embracing a tree.
His figure is caught in twilight and shadows.
His right cheek pressed tight against the trunk
As if in holy prayer
Or quiet contemplation with mother nature.
In the upper left hand corner of the picture
A bird on a branch looks down on him.
Wild flowers form a wreath around his feet,
Leaves cling to his legs.
Silhouetted in the dusk,
His bare back is crisscrossed with a latticework of chains.
Off to the side, standing next to the photographer,
Three men scuff the ground with their boots,
Spit tobacco juice into the dirt,
And in voices barely audible
Talk about boll weevils and the weather.

Strangers

She comes to her in the dark when she least expects her.
Resurrects in thoughts
When she's wide awake listening to the rain.
Her apparition enters when she's wide awake
Tossing and turning to the wind and the lightning strike.
Her presence vanishes and returns
When she's not prepared, caught off guard from impressions
She evokes, old memories conjured up,
Mirage in the shimmering distance,
Recollections she can sense but cannot touch.

Why the persistence after all these years?
What reasons cause
The steadfast heart to connive itself,
Complicate the mind with thoughts
Of someone she barely knew, seldom held?
What logic defies this irrational notion
For their lives only periodically crossed,
Few words exchanged except in passing,
The stuttering, unnatural conversations,
Uncontrollable nervousness her beauty provoked
So unsettling she took her breath away?

The last time the two of them spoke,
A Sunday brunch at a noisy cafe,
Future plans, insecurities, doubts,
Small talk and silence as diners watched
The awkward gestures of ambivalent friends.

And now, in her own small world, tedious
With the years of promises unfulfilled, claustrophobic
Netherworld of middle age and regret, anal academics,
The woman she never became,
The woman she is but does not like
Flat on her back at three o'clock in the morning
Still wondering whatever happened
To those possibilities she once imagined
To be reachable, within her grasp,
As real as the moonlight in her window,

The dim light of the clock on the bedside table,
The subtle breathing of her wife on the pillow right next to her
Unknowing and devout.

Near San Tomás Aquino Creek

Boundaries outline where a table and bed once sat.
Purple pattern on a worn out carpet,
Cemetery of forgotten footsteps.
Copper wires dangle from dead sockets in walls,
Bare walls with dirty smudges and fingerprints
Intersecting cobwebs in the corners.

Not even a note or a forwarding address,
No breadcrumbs leaving a trail.
Invisible spirits of whispers, the only secrets left.
The dulled glass of a dime store mirror
Hangs in a room where gentle hearts once burned
And a child was born.

Solitary vase on a window sill,
Dog-eared pages of a water-stained book,
Single blue hair clip in the back of a closet,
Even the unseen evidence of an open door,
Squeaking creak of a rusted hinge
Has been hushed with the final exit.

Only the aftermath and mustiness remains
Bereft of the accents of old conversations.
No faint trace of flowers lingers in the air,
No exotic aroma of food.
Only a ghost of burnt wood arched a soft halo
On the bricks that frame the fireplace.

Though every now and then on certain days
When the winds are just right,
Enough to bring the senses back into focus,
A vague photograph develops
Of old promises and hopes,
And if one listens long enough to the silence of the self,
The patina can be tasted.

Confession

I should have built bridges for you
Across rust strewn river bottoms,
Fabricated tales of hope
Through grime dulled windows,
Transformed a palm full of pebbles
Into sapphires for your eyes.

I should have combed the dust
Of cluttered antique shops,
Found poetry in colored glass
Of cheap vases,
Gathered up old pictures and frames for you
To take apart and reconstruct.

Everything for your art, water
For your thirst,
I should have been the man you imagined
The qualities a man should be,
Found virtuous ways
To harbor fortitude from faults.

But these are hollow promises,
Whispers to assuage my guilt.
Should haves, did nots,
Failures unraveling in false catharsis,
Brambles upon which I impale myself,
Dishonesty and denial.

Confession is shameless here,
Audacity by your bedside,
Cowardliness in the company
Of your lifeless form,
Quiet bubbling of medicinal tubes,
Silence of your tongue.

There is no sacrifice involved
When words are not returned,
Restitution not demanded.
Compassion's transparent

As the chemical liquid in the vials,
Penitence, unforgiven.

In the darkness of your room
My complicity on its knees,
I've become my own confessor
At the altar of your trauma,
Sacrilege of devotion
Will take a lifetime to absolve.

Sunnybrae

Before the tide pools were paved into parking lots
And the bright lights of the city diminished the starry night.
Before the engineers moved into the bungalows
Of stone cutters and brick masons
And their sons and daughters neatly coifed
Walked the halls and corridors
Where raggedy boys once played
And ran late to the bells:

Before the wrecking balls and eminent domain
Crumbled landmarks into rubble.
Before expectations flattened out
And optimisms collapsed into small concessions
Then finally devoured themselves
As the housing tracts, one after another,
Feasted on the carcass of verdant meadows
And swallowed the furrowed land:

Before the Euclidian pronouncements
And diabolical agendas of shadowy figures
And special interests
Disemboweled ethics on the postmodern altar.
Before the shoulders of the slumbering hills
Were veined with fairways in the name of leisure
And the sweep of panoramic vistas
Were blasted into the bluffs:

Before the views gave way to the gates
And the multiple stories obscured the lakes.
Before the perfumes of the valley
And the sweet and fragrant odors of the canneries
Succumbed to the overload and monoxide
And the python coil of the byways and the freeways
And the traffic's snarling wake
Eviscerated the fields:

Before the pink lungs inhaled the dense stench
Of chemicals, smokestacks billowing
The manufactured odors of business.

Before the sweat and impatience of pedestrians,
Rot of garbage, creosote, cordite,
Acridity of progress overwhelmed
The olfactory ability to comprehend
This pungent industrial incense:

Before litigation and the avarice of premiums
Emptied the parks and the playgrounds
Of make believe and imagination.
Before echo chambers, confirmation bias,
Algorithmic systems, thumbs and emoji instead of tongues,
Distracted drivers crossing lines
Collided the actual and virtual world
Into a chaos of misinformation:

Before the delicate breezes of better days
And the aspirations of idealists
Became the nourishment of insomniacs.
Before the serenity of dirigibles
Floating mysteriously against the sunrise
Gave way to thumping autos
Full of bitterness and rage,
Vocabularies of murder and misogyny:

Before the destitute and dispossessed
Wandered like specters on city streets
And altruism and civic duty
Got laid out on the cooling board.
Before the insecurity of security
And violent individuals and lockdowns
Increased exponentially,
Symbols and symptoms of a deeper disease:

Before the Sunday chimes gathered acolytes in arenas
To hear charismatic preachers
Sell Jesus and the Gospels like Chevrolets,
Their smiles twisted into crooked grins
Of calculations and the knife-points of profit.
Before diatribes and dissonance
Cannibalized the dialogues and civil discourse

And made demagogues out of second-rate intellects:

Before the universe shrank into the palm of a hand
And the horizon dissolved at the tip of the nose.
Before the ancient observation
Of the Roman philosopher Seneca
"That to be everywhere is to be nowhere"
Came upon the present like a plague
And the neighborhoods of once upon a time
Metastasized into silence:

The groves and gardens, ranches and vineyards,
Orchards of pear and apricot, plum, and olive,
Cherry blossoms, clean meandering streams,
Crickets, birdsongs, honeysuckle and rose
Intensified by dusk, the sun-dappled waters
Of lakes and ponds, blushed amethyst of sunsets,
All fed the longing hopes of our mythical youth,
Our romanticized past whose vanishing remains.

Anamnesis

Years ago I passed through after the war.
I'd hitchhiked from the coast
And having been dropped off in the middle of nowhere
I threw my duffel down where the paved road
Sloped into gravel and I spent the night in a barn
On the edge of town.

Waking at dawn I walked a half mile to main street
Past boarded windows, rusty stacks of iron gears
Piled in abstract sculpture,
Greasy plume of a two-bit diner
Evaporating into the mist.

Along the way I passed an elderly couple
Standing in a field of weather worn monuments,
Tilted angles,
Clarities and absolutes of another age
Carved into the railings of a bridge I crossed.
A rickety truck sputtered past,
And a frail looking woman in a long coat
Bowed her frame into the wind.

I paused a bit in the town square
And read the arbitrary names on a bronze plaque,
Listened to a school bell in the distance,
Then pushed east toward a grain elevator
And a solitary steeple, alabaster divinity
Of an airplane's vapor trail, high overhead,
Stuck in my throat.

Postcard

A woman and a girl and a small dog on a leash
Make their way up the street.
From all appearances, a mother and daughter,
The young girl on metal crutches
Awkward gait and dragging leg.

It's an odd scene, this pleasant afternoon,
Carmel by the Sea,
Tourists and villagers, overpriced art,
Stylish clothes far more expensive
Than they're worth.

I feel out of place
In my Jesus and Mary Chain t-shirt,
Scuffed cowboy boots and silver tooth.
Hung over and sipping coffee,
I sit on a bench taking it all in.

The two figures move further apart.
A look of disgust on the mother's face,
"Hurry up!" she snaps, "We're late."

Hands on her hips, she watches her daughter
Struggle up the incline, spastic movements
Side to side, heavy breathing, labored grimace,
The mother's sneer targeted my way
Like a broadcast of buckshot.

Seagulls circling overhead,
Glistening pulse of blue ocean in the distance,
Platinum blonde in a classic Jaguar
Stopped at the crosswalk,
And the young girl inching forward up the slope
Watery-eyed and breathless in the salty wind,
Homesick for Dubuque.

After Hours

Polished oak of the piano, poached ivory of the keys,
When my great aunt growled the blues
She could wake from dusty sleep Rocinante's ghost,
Freeze a deer in its tracks like headlights can,
Move color around a canvas
Better than any painter I ever knew.

The metamorphosis of notes into faces,
Clusters of chords reinterpreting the raw laws
Of nature, she sipped bourbon when she played,
Would have made Mozart blush with her flourishes,
She conjured up images like bite marks
And cut up anyone who took the stage.

Lucky Strike dangling from her lipstick mouth,
Outlandish hat and feather boa,
Hunched shoulders and bony wrists,
Two hands dancing in contrapuntal symbiosis,
Her songs sung the photos of *Let Us Now Praise Famous Men*, reassembled tones into meadows.

My great aunt invoked the spirits of her red dirt past,
Depression migrations, tobacco roads,
Rolled slow dirges mournful as the homeless,
Honky-tonk and boogie-woogie, improvisational jazz,
Juke-joint smoke, epistemology of her roots,
Lifetime played in ragtime and euphonious riffs.

Prima Facie

They called you crazy Mary.
On nights when they were bored, tired of tormenting
All God's creatures great and small,
They searched for you downtown, down side streets,
On the twinkling bright lights of the boulevard.
They'd roll up, and roll down the windows of their cars
Honk their horns and shout, taunt you with hoots,
Howl at you like some dogs do at fire trucks.

They had it down to a fine art, among other things in those days,
Like setting girls up in graveyards on summer nights,
But what about you?
Where did you live and who was the bride
Who brought you home to the cradle?
Who was the groom who tucked you in?
What did the neighbors think
Peering out from their doorways,
The mailman who never stopped to talk?
When did your bones and breasts and the sway of your hips
Separate the woman from the child?
How long ago did the music abandon your throat
And leave you with only the grunts and groans
That delighted them so?

Slouched down in their low-slung cars cruising for blood,
What did they see in themselves in you way back then
That not even their mothers recognized?

Rosabel's Tio In The San Joaquin Valley

He monitors temperatures in the grove
From sunset to sunrise.
A fragrant aroma of citrus mixes
With an acrid blend of chemicals
Whose names he cannot pronounce.
His thoughts drift in and out,
Recollect his youth in Guanajuato,
Christmas memories, novenas, orphans,
Focus on the antics of a spotted dog
That ambles beside him.

Looking up at stars he fondles a small cross
On a silver chain around his neck,
Brings it to his lips as a gesture of faith,
Wishes he was back in bed
And the soft breathing of his wife.
Inhaling the bite of the night frost
He squints at ornaments and candy-colored lights
Strung like a necklace around a house,
Counts three blessings for each of his children.

Disconnected from the earth in December's dark
He dreams of home and his father,
Prays for those who bleed and give birth
In the fertile soil of the fields.
Hates that he understands
The atrocity of women and men
Treated like machinery, replaceable parts,
Hands that sow what others reap,
The puzzling chasm that lies between
That which is holy and merely human.

Out Of Limits

Skateboarders, sidewalk surfers,
Banking, lipping, kicking,
Getting air off the high side,
Gliding, sliding, thrashing
In power drive down the face.
Coyote howling in the distance,
Freight train rumbling by.
Bigmouth bass
Busting the glass of calm water
In the summer night behind the dam.
Moonbeams in the eyes
Of young women and young men.
Rock n' roll radio, rap, country twang
Pulsating from the open doors
Of a four-wheel drive.
Cracking laugh of beer bottle
On white cement, slab of concrete,
Virgin canvas for spray paint,
Graffiti monument.
Jive talk, buzz cuts, purple Mohawks,
Baggy shorts, puffs of blunts,
Artists, athletes, students.
The sky is bright tonight overhead,
Veritable Van Gogh adagio
Of violet indigo and starlight.
Like a poet once said,
It's street corner college, man,
Basquiat and Kerouac, Tupac,
Madonna come to life.
Youth doing
What only youth must do, does best,
Revolt against the weight.

Witness

As the object of your attention
I've learned by rote
What it means to see stars,
Have been dragged by my hair
Around the house and down stairs.

I have felt the sting
Of the blistering backhand,
Have worn the black and blue marks
Of broken promises and vows,
The calling cards of the mad.

My pink nightgown stained with blood,
I have screamed quietly
So as not to wake the children,
The menace of your presence
Ever the constant sentry.

When the court demands
Why did I kill you
I shall take a deep breath and stand,
Wipe away my tears
And spit out the words of that Jefferson man.

Healing

Last night lightning killed my daughter's horse.
I found it this morning stiff as a board
As if it were asleep among the flowers in the field.
I bound it up with chains
While the spring rains came fast and cold.
My wife told me she'd break the news to our only child
That life's lessons can be hard
And that sometimes prayers don't make a difference,
Don't mean a thing.
I busied myself with work and later in the day
Drove into town to see about the tractor in the shop.
After dinner, while my wife cleaned up,
I sat on the couch with our daughter
And watched the fire dance shadows on stained bricks.
She asked me to read with her from a book of poems
Her grandmother had given to her for Christmas.
She said here, this one, and leaned her head against my shoulder,
Her soft breathing in rhythm with mine
As we spoke each verse.

Sometimes

The high scream of the metallic saws is soothing.
Steam and piston clatter of jack hammers
Busting up chunks of cement and stone
Fit well sometimes with my disposition.
Thunderous roar of jet planes lifting off from runways,
Sirens, arguments of neighbors, honking horns,
Squealing sound of burnt rubber and brakes,
Sometimes the rusty hinges of warehouse doors
Are curiously more comforting to me
Than the glistening, glassy waters of dusk
Cerebral and calm.
Every now and then when tranquility is simply too severe
A trauma to endure,
Drone of machinery, factory whistles and fireworks,
Tornado rumble of the freight train
Soothe me with their nervous edges,
Balance my equilibrium.

Clamor and din of the frenetic city,
Electrified hum of the pulsating and blazing neon,
In certain moments the claustrophobic cacophony of the subway
Choreographed with the discordant diesel
Combustion of the smoking busses
Unfold as some kind of surrealistic
Balanchine to my senses.
Early morning banging of corrugated trash cans
Slammed against the sides of brick buildings,
Fog horns of outward bound ships
In the long hours before dawn,
Sometimes the booming bass drone throbbing from radios and autos
Are infinitely more embracing to my psyche
Than the stillness of wet woods
In the aftermath of a storm.

Indeed, on some days I guess I don't suffer
Silence too well for too long,
Instead preferring the company and conversations
Of reckless men and edgy women in rowdy bars,
The fellowship of the streetwise and two-fisted

Contemplating philosophical conundrums
Unknown to Kierkegaard.
And occasionally when peace and quiet
Are simply not aesthetic enough,
Are anathema to the heart,
I seek solace out open windows
Down to where the black rivers intersect
And the manmade volcanoes in the bellies
Of the foundries and the steel mills
Release their clouds of fume and smoke
Into the dark meadows of the night,
And my spirit disconnects, tranquilized and transcendent,
And floats on the glow of the molten light
Radiating to the stars.

Silhouette Of Mato Tipila

Panoramic plains ache with the memories of countless voices,
Wagon rut and will, desperate destinations, voyages
Fondly recollected or ill-begotten, whispers of turning wheel
And oxen, bedraggled dreamers dragging children.

Immensity of plateaus and star filled heavens,
Endless stream of broken dialects heavy with burdens,
Wilderness of seasons above this weariness of hopes,
Invisible diaries of lost generations resurrected on the wind.

Migrant ocean without wave save for the subtle heaving of sighs,
Constellations of memories of a thousand forgotten days,
Collective brunt of resolutions whose nameless fates
Resolved dying futures long ago.

Shimmering gleam of landscapes holding mysteries in their vistas,
Geomorphic provinces in the salty squinted distance,
Dusky mountains silhouetted in the afterglow of sunsets,
Dazzling expanse of dawns and their beckoning arms.

Undulant valleys and brilliantine green of verdant meadows,
Earthen nebula of cerulean skies, copper slated canyons,
Flaming gorges coral blazed and fired in amethyst and pinks,
Jaw-gaping rivers of rumbling froth and emerald.

The dusty bones of Jesuits, unmarked graves of immigrations far removed,
The bison ghosted prairies full of families without names,
Manifestations that ancient cultures prophesied with smoke,
Conjured from their visions this dispiriting flood.

Spirits of sacred ancestors trapped within their throats,
Lakota and Cheyenne, Crow and Arapaho, hand prints on the hindquarters
Of painted ponies, obsidian eyes of silent observers,
Prayers and offerings at Bear Butte.

But still the snaking line, rivulet to torrent as far as the oblivion scope
Of the sweltering desert stretches, omnipotent current of inevitable change,
Efflorescence trampled under hoof, circling predations of scavenger birds,
Steel tracks of catastrophe glistening in the sun.

Pulsing settlement of virgin land, Manifest Destiny justifying purpose,
Pandemic thrust of missionary crusades, machine in the garden,
Prophetic tales of cause and effect, plunder and pillage,
The elders spoke, apocalyptic weeping of their eclipsed hearts.

Before Panel 17W—Line 3

They became the daily sounds of children
Bicycling and walking to schools,
Pulse and pause of high-pitched voices,
Cheering crowds of the baseball stadium,
Sacred intervals of the monastery bells
Blessing the prayers of the cloistered nuns
Who lived in devotion behind pink walls.

They learned early to avoid the vicious dogs
That prowled the alleyways and the fields,
Explored the family farms and ranches,
Hunted for pheasant and jack rabbit,
Ran scared from cranky blasts of rock salt,
Hiked the craggy banks of the tangled creek
Late for dinner and gone for miles.

They lounged on the grass in the summer heat,
Huddled together in winter's cold, talking,
Smoking cigarettes and pot, embellishing tales
Of lost love and adventure, confessing secrets
To absolve their sins, laughing themselves
Deep into the comforting darkness of the park
Until the light of dawn breathed in their bones.

They took wild rides in hopped up cars,
Raced chopped out bikes like land-locked meteors
Up and down the neon boulevards, tree-lined
Roads snaking along the sunburned countryside,
They red-lined the long curving asphalt,
Black ribbon of freedom that traced the ocean's edge
From the avenues all the way down to the lane.

They stood on the precipice of the lighthouse cliff
Inhaling dreams, the emerald green sea sparkling
Pure glass, the turquoise glazed California sky,
Bright Pacific beading on the bronzed angelic
Bodies of their girlfriends, salt spray and wave crash
Beckoning them to dive head first into the swells
And the bold beautiful blue deep of amen.

That Year

Affirmation of the news reverberated
Through the streets of the small town,
Kept the window lights burning late.

With every retelling the telling changed
As rumors beget the myths
Until myths became the truth.

The following day in the coffee shops
And cafes, along the leave cluttered
Lanes full of children walking to school

Business as usual broke the dawn,
Optimism raised the flag. Church on Sunday
Saw no increase in the crowds

And the sun glowed and set upon the lawns
And the gentle breezes eased the routines
Of the ordinary and mundane.

Few faces said that anything was wrong.
And when Christmas came that year
Families gathered and the pageant played,

The choirs sang the sacred songs
And little kids squealed with delight
As they opened the gifts that Santa brought.

Another year came and went, more businesses
Closed down, and once again the roiling river
Rose up, capricious in its intent.

Closing Up Shop

Wilderness of expectations, half-baked ideas,
Dramatic anatomy of unspoken hopes,
He nursed his bloody knuckles and bruised bones
In the twilight din of a damp auto shop,
Sat in a cloud of blue smoke
Curling up from a gnarled hand.

Aspirations that never materialized,
What a stark realization it must have been,
Random chance of opportunities
That came and went, unspoken vows,
Bargained convictions long since gone
Time worn flat, smooth as stone.

He toiled like a plow horse through two wars,
Frozen December in Belgium, Chosin,
Cracked images of weary men,
Tarnished medals in a bureau drawer,
Recollections he seldom spoke about,
Waved off with the shake of his head.

Demons and burdens manifested
As the fourteen stations themselves,
My uncle lived vicariously
In the shadows of our lives, through our children,
Came into our homes at holiday gatherings
A quiet man and his ghosts.

Faded sign on his dark garage,
Screws and bolts of unfinished business,
Puddles of oil and metallic scents, dust and mold,
Down on my knees in iridescent grease,
I stare at a photograph found in a closet
Of a wide-eyed boy holding up a fish.

Ephemeral

Looking beyond the boundaries of our safe places,
Acquaintances who question not our weaknesses
But accept us unequivocally as members of a family
Related as if by blood, but perhaps even closer
Than those siblings who oftentimes know less of us
Than those who share our most secret intimacies,
Once we travel outside to breach the broader earth
Of continental states, distant shores, foreign countries,
We discover that many truths contradict our own,
Numerous inconsistencies shatter our complacencies,
How the multi-faceted elements of mortal existence
Are not as simple or as deductible as we oftentimes
Assumed from the safe haven of our perspectives,
The solacing comfort of our prejudices and biases,
And we understand at that point in our small lives
That everything below the stars and the ever-changing moon
The synapses of all natural things and human life
Are interconnected in the graceful and violent
Fits and pauses of evolution's relentless reinventions
And at that moment in our personal examinations
In our earnest efforts to comprehend the world
As something much greater than us but a part of us
We understand with insight and epiphany
That everywhere is nowhere and somewhere all at once
And everyone we meet, we meet again ourselves,
And every place we leave, was every place a home.

Hope Springs Eternal

Each semester I tell my students that it's the small moments that matter most.
Whether or not they listen, is another matter.
As students, they are more concerned with practical aspects of the course:
Is the final cumulative? How many absences are too many? Do you care
If we bring food? Do you offer extra-credit?
Do we have to purchase the books?

I emphasize that everything is fodder for the historian and that, as
William Faulkner once wrote, "The past is never dead. It's not even past."
But as they fiddle with their phones or whisper to their neighbor I never
Lose sight of the fact that I see myself sitting in this same class decades ago
Wondering how I might get the number of the sweetheart to my left.
In their faces full of boredom and expectation, I watch myself perform.

I often hear people say that critical thinking is imperative
And that colleges are failing to equip their students
With the tools to cope with the modern world.
I must confess, I do not share that self-righteous sentiment, as the value
Of education, in and of itself, is probative and every discipline demands
A different process of thought all critical in their intent.

But I digress. I try to impress upon my students that marks are less
Important than knowledge and that knowledge is many times
Not learned in a classroom such as this. Degrees fulfill pragmatic ends,
But it's the living that matters most. It's that road trip taken
At the spur of the moment, each and every day of our lives,
That demands of us our full attention, grades be damned.

Alice Drive

Every year he grew angrier, mowed his perfect grass with fiercer intentions,
Kept the window shades drawn a little longer in the day.
Hunched over the wheel of his truck with more steadfast resolve,
Seldom waved goodbye to his wife in the doorway.

Every decade the flowers and shrubs grew higher, paint faded
Around the eves and shutters, smoke spiraled less frequently
From his chimney, the pleasant odors of his Sunday barbecues
No longer perfumed the neighborhood.

Rarer the days and evenings when the ballgame could be heard
As he tinkered in his garage on the first car he ever bought.
How the seasons came and the seasons went
Until his sparkling pool had lost its brilliance.

After his funeral, I stood with his son on the brick patio
That our fathers set down, stood chatting in the late afternoon
As he recalled his dad, the odd behaviors of a peculiar man
Who'd lost his own father before he was ten.

I asked him why his father was always angry,
Screamed at kids who ran across his lawn,
Kept toys and balls that had been tossed into his garden,
Rumored to have poisoned the neighbor's dog?

He told me his pop hadn't been the same since the accident
When he pulled a girl from a flaming car,
How he sat with her burned body on the side of the road
And held her head in his lap as a crowd looked on.

He said it was a relief that his father was gone
Because he took his demons with him to eternal rest,
A better place where even the wicked can be forgiven.
I shook his hand and walked away in search of my wife and children.

I wandered across his yard, felt the sun upon my back, inhaled the deep
Heat of the early summer eve, thought about our purposes and where
We find them, how we hide our pain and compromise ambitions,
And with a child in my arm, knelt down and touched his grass.

Chain-link Fence

Passersby and visitors, strangers, reporters,
Relatives fold paper flowers and mementos
Into the honeycomb of the chain-link fence.
Tie ribbons onto wire, tape poems to poles,
Paste locks of hair onto photographs
Wrapped in angels made of foil.
Morning, noon, and night the vigil evolves
The guilt-ridden who survived, tourists,
The inquisitive and curious,
Weak knees, helplessness, countenance transfixed,
Palms and faces pressed against the barrier,
Introspection above the hole.
Low whispers barely audible,
Prayers to the beloved, Eucharist
For the grieving, comfort for the anguish.
Our penitence an epitaph,
Speechlessness, invocation of the lost,
Liturgy of tears, consecration of rubble.
Without pause, the requiem,
The mournful eulogy continues,
Watery eyes like reflecting pools or grottos,
Blank stares articulating silence,
Inability of the living to sanctify with words
The blasphemy of the aftermath.

In The Aftermath Of Ashes

He accelerates over the Golden Gate Bridge
Haunted with the heavy scent
Of his father's funeral.
He speeds away from the tears of his brothers
That some fragrance will remember
Years from now,
Those recollections the living retain,
Indelible burdens of our compassion.
With stoic condolences and mourning bells
Still echoing in his ears,
He rolls down the window to catch his breath,
To hear the flood of the rain swept road.

Squinting into the glistening headlights
Of oncoming cars,
He pushes north to the northwest coast,
Toward the homes of his children
And the grave of his wife.
Through small towns and at coffee shops
He collects himself,
Chats with strangers at truck stops,
Bathes his questions in the sacred water
Of the midnight ocean.
In quiet communion he walks alone, barefoot,
Down by the wharves and the fishing boats.

He strains to comprehend
The mystical language of shimmering seals,
Black and shiny pearls
Perched on the pinnacles of barnacled rocks.
He races north, proud but lost,
His turquoise surfboard strapped on top,
Mingus, Dolphy, Davis, and Coltrane
Soothing him with their visions.
Their intense rhythms of bop and blues
Painting landscapes more powerful
Than any poetry he's ever heard.
Swallowed in the darkness of the indigo night,
Their timeless art, a perfect companion.

As he crosses raging rivers of no return,
The a cappella choir of the hypnotic storm
Thunders from the balcony of late December.
The vagabond silhouette of his battered truck
Throws a desperate shadow
Against the witness of the cliffs.
Doubts and bloodshot eyes
Compensate for a compass,
Familiar failure of words guiding him blindly
Through canyons of fog,
Personal thoughts of insignificance, like live wires,
Raw emotions like the roar of the breakers
Crashing into the coves.

Weight of guilt upon his shoulders,
Tattoos of shattered dreams concealed
In a graveyard of invisible scars,
He moves across the unmarked border.
Beneath a sentry of stars and a crescent moon
He drives his heart into the arms of dawn.
Clearing his head with the pine odors of Oregon,
He struggles to remember.
Returning home with broken promises to repair,
Misgivings to forgive,
With the ashes of his father in hand
He knocks on his mother's door.

Noa's Savta

She still sees her,
Wrinkled fingers kneading dough on a wooden board.
Silver hair like wire, thick stockings
And tired black shoes. Choir in her gentle eyes.
Flowery fragrance of the perfume she wore.
Soft sounds of Vivaldi and Chopin
Crackling from the tiny mouth
Of a transistor radio.
Like some elegant portrait from Caravaggio,
She still sees her, a small child at the hem of her dress,
Her quiet smile, her patience, her heavy hips,
Glint of a gold band, an old reminder.
She still remembers
The comforting scent of baking,
Warm cider simmering on a stove.
Her mother's mother in the alcove of a kitchen,
Glasses riding on the tip of her nose,
The grace of a saint in the late afternoon.
She still recalls the autumn light
Illuminating the room with a translucent glow,
The tender way she placed bread on her tongue,
Stigmata of pale blue numbers on her floured arm
Bleeding through.

Sanctuary

January: We're running late. Ice crunches beneath our feet.
I'd like to say we are headed off to be born, this first month
Of the new year, but that is not the case. A doctor's office
Awaits our arrival and perhaps news that the fresh start
We anticipated will have to be delayed until the lake thaws,
Until the spring rains make everything right and days warm.

February: We lay in bed all day long in one another's arms
Listening to the wind bend trees in the flower barren yard.
The neighbor's dog howled up a storm tethered to a chain
And the phone rang in the middle of the night for no reason.
You asked me if I still felt the same way I did when we first met
As I bathed your aching bones in the fragrant water of a bath.

March: Our second child came rushing home from school
To inform us that Ansel Adams' photographs reminded her
Of grandpa's paintings that she saw last week in the gallery.
We spread out a wrinkled map on the living room floor
And reminisced about all of the places we had lived,
Debated the merits of keeping relatives at arm's length.

April: We paddled out at dawn hoping to surf a few sets
Before heading off to work. Icy water ran down our necks
Until our wetsuits heated our bodies to achieve the perfect balance
Between our flesh and the frigid Pacific. The anonymity
Of our place in the universe put into proper perspective
And wild gratitude gave us goose bumps as we paddled in.

May: Despite the warnings, the lowering came quickly,
Our new home in Oklahoma was shattered above our heads.
We stumbled out into the green gray day and the aftermath,
Mouths agape, we stood with others in our neighborhood,
Looked around at a scene that weathermen would describe
As a war zone or lunar landscape, like Dresden or Nagasaki.

June: You complained that the pain had migrated deeper
Like a dull throbbing or a distant voice that you could not
Answer no matter how hard you tried. We sat for hours
In the tick-tock tedium of the white office, only a gown

Covering the curves and soft meadows of the girl I loved,
Your sweet secret that tasted like peaches to my tongue.

July: Our kids ran willy-nilly through our front yard
Waving sparklers whose brightly colored arcs reminded me
Of lightning or the boardwalk in Santa Cruz or the parking
Lot carnivals that came around when we were young,
My father welding in our garage with sparks dancing
Across the floor, his darkened silhouette god-like and frightening.

August: The sweltering sunlight was comforting on our skin.
We took long walks late into the firefly nights, giggled like kids
Again riding the Ferris wheel at the local amusement park,
Drank lemonade from a little girl's umbrella covered stand.
The stars were beautiful in the sky, distant and untouchable,
Sparkling asterisms casting light on our ordinary lives.

September: The crepe myrtles were finishing their bloom
And despite the vatic proclamations of political analysts
We looked forward to the new school year and the students
Returning with all of their eclectic and irrepressible style.
We took a balloon ride over the New Mexico landscape
And became luminescent in that land of enchantment.

October: For Halloween we both dressed like Daffy Duck.
At your boss's party I walked into a sliding glass door
After too many shots. You laughed so hard you snorted,
Laughed so long your stomach hurt, your eyes watered,
You lost your breath. We dove into the pool at two a.m.
Two cartoon characters, water rolling off our backs.

November: This month, not April, was the cruelest of months.
We took ourselves apart like puzzles, folded hopes
Into origami as if the mere act of thinking good thoughts
Would somehow make the platitudes appear less ominous.
Both you and I trying to make sense of second opinions,
We drove across the mesa in Black Mesa anxious and lost.

December: The art of haiku is an ancient art, let me practice
On you, I whispered, as I came up behind you in the kitchen,
The two girls setting the table, the dogs, as always, just happy
To be alive, the doorbell ringing and the first friends arriving
With wine and gifts all the way from Chico and Tucumcari,
Snow falling in the twilight, luminarias lighting our walk.

House

Apologies were never enough.
Words flew like sparks from her mouth,
Her arms flapping up and down
Like some apoplectic bird.

Fixed in the cross hairs
Of her cubist eyes,
Her smeared lipstick
Angled her face into a cockeyed shape.
It was advisable to not say a word
But bob and flinch, hunch and cower.
Grit the teeth
Amidst the knickknacks
Swept from their places,
The shattered glass,
Interminable silences
Like white-hot steam.
Ride it out the best a child could
Within the confines of the cage,
Until rage flattened to tears
And the claws retracted.

Only then was it safe
To venture a breath,
Feign a posture of guilt
With a downward glance
And tip-toe past the beast
Through the rancor and the ashes,
Escape into the fields
And the kisses of the rain.

Other Side Of The Tracks

Angular and ornamental
In its postmodern aesthetic,
It's a well-appointed house
Full of contradictions, shadows and light.
In the open space of the great room
A blue marlin and rhino head
Are mounted on a wall above a Paolo Buffa desk.
A sizzling aroma of garlic
Perfumes a conversation involving immigration
And resorts. Muted trumpet of Miles Davis
In the background, a playful Löwchen
Frolics among the children
With a purple dog bone in its mouth.
In an alcove framed with redwood timbers,
A floor to ceiling aquarium
Is filled with the glow of exotic fish.
A perfectly coiffed woman,
Bangles dangling from her arm,
Points to magnificent hues of salmons
Blues and pinks in halo above a ridge,
Sunset gleams in jeweled tones
Washing across the porch.
In the foyer, a man lifts a sherry
And in a barely audible voice
Remarks to no one in particular,
"This is what's it's all about."
Track-lit and to his left,
An original Matisse hangs above a hutch
Full of Zuni pottery and a Joseph Cornell.
Coming out of the kitchen, the hostess clinks a spoon
Against Waterford glass, its elegant note
Bringing silence to the evening.
Her friends and parents look to her,
Her husband smiling broadly
Wondering what she intends,
Blissful eyes twinkling
And a bit watery from the wine,
The inviting scent of warm food
That has been placed upon the table,

No one says a thing, only anticipation.
Only the rising wind
Whispering perfectly against the windows,
Only the antiphonal coolness
Of Coltrane on a groove.

Frida

Imperfections transformed into trademarks,
Wounds became style.
Imaginations fired in the kiln heart
Of shattered passions and rapture,
Self-portraits mirrored
In the eyes looking inward, looking out.

Introspections fused into symbols,
Variations into contrast.
Deeper secrets inside of illuminated truths,
Substance below surface.
Metaphors sparked from pensive strokes,
Confessions forged on metal canvas.

Sable brushes, magical realism of her pallet,
Contrived date of birth
To mark the birth of the revolution.
Earthy and vivid hues infused her realizations,
Epistolary conversations
Carried on within herself.

Bonfire

White smoke billows up from the burning.
Caught in the updraft of the chill wind
Unethical imaginations flicker in the air,
Transparent ashes denounced as lacking a moral center,
Wisps of language, pages of books, unsacred photographs,
Satanic verse and blasphemies spiral skyward into the dusk.

Sober folks sway back and forth, arms around shoulders,
Eyes focused on the oak-stoked fire.
Gospel melodies, chorales, evangelistic hymns
Signifying the river, the child, the cross,
Witness uplifted from the smolder of poems,
Process of purification, absolution of paper.

Heads bowed in deference, exhilarated and exhausted,
The gathering listens as the pastor
Condemns the embers with a few final words, an amen,
Bids goodnight to the compliant crowd,
These killers of light who return to their homes
Scattering stones from their pockets.

Archaeologist

Harbor lights sparkle.
Arcing spider explosions of fireworks
Illuminate the intoxication of gazing eyes.
These are the traces that I remember
Twenty thousand miles behind,
Thirty summers into the future.
Water-stained album full of photographs,
Yellowed envelopes filled with letters,
Frayed ribbon.

Mental images linger, incidental mementos
Whose weight or unimportance fluctuate
According to mood, time of day,
Perfume scented on a passing stranger.
Conversations overheard reawakening
Slumbering imperfections of yesterdays,
Subtle ecstasies and burdens,
Dialogues and consequences
Reconstructed, misconstrued.

It was a violent year of assassinations,
Omnipotent insignificance.
Flotsam and jetsam of failed revolutions,
Imagined tomorrows already dead.
We stood on the bridge long past midnight
Unsuspecting victims of ill-fated devotions,
Fog horn soundings of rocking ships
Heading out to god knows where,
Swirling wakes of impermanence.

And now, here in the attic, romantic nostalgia
Of a middle-aged man alphabetizing indexes
Rearranging books and albums on a shelf,
Dusting off old artifacts with the same unassailable
Faith that everything has a purpose.
Circle rings of growth, non-linear memories,
Adages and anecdotes, chimeras that play tricks,
Brushed antiquities dissolving in the hand
Enigmatic and mute.

Among Other Things

In a perfect world the high road never disappeared
In a puff of smoke.
Santana begins every Saturday night,
Ad infinitum, with Soul Sacrifice, the Woodstock version,
And Samba Pa Ti.
My siblings and I and my childhood friends
Fall asleep gazing up at Mojave Desert ceilings,
Crystal clear Yosemite skies
Beneath moonlight and stars,
Taste the winds of the Great Plains as if they were pie.
Dawn patrol welcomes each new day
As we paddle out beyond the breakers
To the glassy green peace of an emerald sea.
That kid taking a twelve gauge and his life
Was nothing but a lie that gossip spread,
While N. Scott Momaday arrives for dinner,
Never late because there is no late,
Articulates an exegesis on *House Made of Dawn*.
Harper Lee leans back with her elbows on the grass
And talks to us and Gao Xingjian about recipes and fame.
Arbeit macht frei was simply a figment
Of someone's imagination.
The passage that Oppenheimer quoted from the Bhagavad Gita
Pertained to something other than human shadows
Burned on stone.
The doom-hard eyes of convicts
And the strung-out frames of freckled face girls
Never became the nightmare of the so-called dream.
That the gouache paintings and montages of Romare Bearden
Are still so fresh and wet we can smell the brush strokes.
The hermeneutical inquiries into ancient texts
Reveal something more profound
Than more questions about questionable faiths.
The notion that the centre cannot hold
Was merely a false alarm.
That Kon Ichikawa and Georgia O'Keeffe
With Dorothea Lange in tow
Skip to My Lou my darling up to our door and knock.
Rose of Sharon, frozen in time, becomes us all,

Offers up what she has to give
In the late shadows of the barn and smiles mysteriously.
That light radiates from every pore, continually,
And Herodotus from here to eternity and the great beyond
Stops spinning in his grave.

In The Shadow Of The Mission And The Monastery

No women spoke of Michelangelo and no two roads diverged.
Nothing slouched toward Bethlehem to be born.
In our small town the boys grew numb and drank hard,
And the girls endured the expectations and limitations of the post-war world.

Not a single thing depended upon a red wheelbarrow in the yard
And the portraits of our parents could not be discerned in convex mirrors.
Walking out into the evenings, practical concerns infused their conversations
Not the fractured syntax of dream songs.

Our community was a contradiction, not a wasteland,
And there lived no aged ploughmen or hollow men or wealthy women
Who wrote villanelles that claimed losing was an art but no disaster.
Heartbreak on our street was an indiscriminate visitor.

The daily ordinary routines that constituted survival
Provided no time to pause or stop for anything, much less death.
There were hardly moments for quiet thought or rest
And there was no escape for the weary to some Coney Island of the mind.

Everyone we loved dove headfirst into the wreck.
There existed no myths of devotion save for Sundays and Holy Communion.
No bitter angels stood on corners on our street, and if those we admired
Did not go gentle into that good night, no one knew.

There was no paradise to be lost within this square mile,
Only the living that life served up to press and challenge the sweet will.
These are the impressions I fathom still,
The river of heaven that rose and fell, the wild irises along the block.

Last Respects At The Grandparents' Farm

Gather up some earth in the palm of your hand
And rub it between your fingers. Savor its scent
And its nurturing essence, how it quietly contains
The stories of your grandfather and the wind.

Embrace the blue hour of the eventide,
Song of the migrating geese in perfect form
Heading south beyond the whispering trees,
Beyond the tales your grandmother shared.

Wade into the river, the cool water on your skin,
Its eddies hold mysteries, heartfelt confessions
Of all of the lovers who have strolled its banks,
Keeps the secrets of the dead safe and sound.

Listen to the night and the soft dialogue of stars,
Walk back into the arms of those who have passed,
The woman and man who gave your mother breath
And the light inside of you that became your life.

Mirrors

They didn't need de Kooning to conceptualize their persona,
These refugees from broken marriages and ne'er-do-wells,
Sisters of Manzanar and Tule Lake, Heart Mountain,
Field weary offspring of Zapata's revolution.
Daughters of daughters of shadows
Who stole across the border,
Widows of Normandy and Korea,
Orphans of the Great Depression.

Ordinary gals, small-town girls
Unfolding in clarity like cactus flowers,
Empathetic eyes like anthologies
Of accumulated suffering or cruel truths,
Paint-stained hair from painting rooms,
Their unruly curls and bright bandanas,
Candy apple of their fingernails.

In the antiseptic infirmaries
Of machinery and dilation,
They birthed our wrinkled faces into a patchwork world
Of housing tracts and orchards,
Chicken farms, silicon corporations,
Sheltered our tiny bodies
In the harbors of their skirts.

Work weathered women defined by accents,
Aromas of chorizo, linguica, soupish,
Sukiyaki and Chianti wine, Portuguese bread,
Garlic on their breath and hands.
Scars of hysterectomies, Caesarean sections,
Thyroid operations,
Stitches in time as stark as their fragrance.

Too saintly to be pious,
They wore their faith on delicate chains,
Virgin Mary and crucifix around their necks,
Worried over rosaries in dim lit bedrooms,
Darkened sanctuaries, stained glass shrines,
Flipped tarot at kitchen tables,

Intuition and prophecies.

Visions recall those sweltering evenings
They watered lawns and visited,
Arms folded beneath their breasts,
Miasma of their worries dissolved in the company
Of others like themselves,
Mothers of mercy
Seeking solace and penitence.

These desolation angels
Who suffered the sober verities
Of feckless dreamers, hard-scrabble men,
Roughnecks and lost causes,
Sweethearts called husbands, best friends,
Childhood companions they gave up trying
Or continued to love.

We inherited their virtues,
Endured the burdens of their bloodlines,
Unraveled from their parables
Exotic shores we could not afford,
Vacations we seldom took.
Watched as time broke their hearts
In diabolical and creative ways
Unimaginable and unforgiven.

And now in diaries and photographs,
In one way conversations,
In our sign language and our silence,
In the noctilucent night of our aging imaginations,
We conjure them up in recipes and tales
Sacrosanct spirits we claim as ourselves,
Fabled amnesia as only children can.

Beyond The Reach

Pink and orange dusk settles like the pastel paintings
Of the old woman on the bench.
Below the overlook of the lighthouse cliff,
Surfers rise up and down
On the swells of the early evening glass.
Concession stands are all closed up
And umbrellas and ice chests have been toted away
By drunken sunburned suburbanites.
Seaweed wraps around the ankles
And a little girl flies a kite at the shoreline edge.
From one end of the boardwalk to the other,
Music from the Loof Carousel
And screams from the roller coaster
Are carried on the cool breeze.
On the street above the river mouth
A hard looking blonde on a Harley,
Blue teardrop at the corner of her eye,
Chats up a skinny kid with freckles
Holding a skateboard.
By the railroad tracks and steel bridge
A tourist snaps photographs
Of two homeboys flashing signs.
On the sacred sand of the ancient beach
As waves break in and wash back out,
Salty dogs and stoners interact
With frisbee throwers and athletes in bikinis.
In the waning glow of the summer sky
Hovering gulls circle endlessly,
Battered old pier still stands,
Fishermen and fisherwomen
Going home to their wives and husbands
Stories much wiser than words,
And beyond the reach, glistening against the sunset,
Pods of gray whales migrate south,
Halos over their weathered humps and blow spouts,
Immutable beauty of their ocean journey
Numinous and sublime.

James Hochtritt grew up in a working-class neighborhood in Santa Clara, California located in the San Francisco Bay Area. The history and physical landscape as well as the multiethnic and multiracial population of the region had a significant influence on his conscious and subconscious development as a poet.

The same could be said about the two dozen or so men and women with whom he formed friendships between 1958-1972 in the Santa Clara Valley. The bonds they forged remain as strong today as the day they first met.

Leaving home at the age of 18, he went on to live in Chico, San Diego, Saratoga, San Jose, and Fresno, California in addition to New York City, as well as Norman and Midwest City, Oklahoma. He worked a wide variety of blue collar and minimum wage jobs to support a life of wanderlust and self-discovery.

He eventually earned a BA in American studies, a BA in history, as well as an MA and Ph.D. in American history with a focus on cultural and social history. Those disciplines allowed him to fully understand what William Faulkner meant when he wrote, "The past is never dead. It's not even past."

During his three decade career in the college classroom, he taught African American, American Indian, and American history to thousands of students who came through his courses. He learned as much from those diverse men and women as hopefully they learned from him.

Although he has been a featured poet at poetry readings in both California and Oklahoma, this is his first published collection of poetry.

www.ingramcontent.com/pod-product-compliance
Lightning Source LLC
Chambersburg PA
CBHW030059170426
43197CB00010B/1588